Sporting Superstars

Fantastic Fact File

Keith Gaines

OXFORD
UNIVERSITY PRESS

Great Clarendon Street, Oxford OX2 6DP

Oxford University Press is a department of the University of Oxford.
It furthers the University's objective of excellence in research, scholarship,
and education by publishing worldwide in

Oxford New York

Auckland Bangkok Buenos Aires Cape Town Chennai
Dar es Salaam Delhi Hong Kong Istanbul Karachi Kolkata
Kuala Lumpur Madrid Melbourne Mexico City Mumbai Nairobi
São Paulo Shanghai Singapore Taipei Tokyo Toronto

with an associated company in Berlin

British Library Cataloguing in Publication Data

Data available

ISBN 0 19 917527 6

10 9 8 7 6 5 4 3 2 1

Inspection Pack (nine different titles) ISBN 0 19 917535 7
Guided Reading Pack (six of the same title) ISBN 0 19 917852 6
Class Pack ISBN 0 19 917536 5

Acknowledgements

The publisher would like to thank the following for permission to reproduce
photographs:

Allsport: p 15 (*top*); Allsport/Tony Duffy: p 23 (*top*); Allsport/Mike Hewitt: p 24;
Allsport/Hulton Deutsch: p 7 (*bottom*); Allsport/IOC Olympic Museum: pp 12, 16
(*top left*), 16 (*bottom left*); Allsport/Steve Powell: p 21 (*main*); Allsport/Ben
Radford: p 3; Associated Press: pp 8 (*right*), 14, 15 (*bottom*), 17 (*top*), 20 (*bottom*),
25 (*top*), 28, 29; BBC Picture Library: pp 8 (*left*), 25 (*bottom*); Corbis/Bettmann:
pp 11, 13 (*both*); Corbis/Tony Sapiano: p 21 (*inset*); Daily Mail 8.8.2001: p 5
(*bottom right*); Empics: pp 4 (*top*), 10 (*top*); Empics/Ross Kinnaird: p 26 (*bottom*),
title page; Keith Gaines Collection: pp 16 (*bottom right*), 18; Golf Monthly Feb.
2002: p 5 (*bottom left*); Hulton Archive: pp 17 (*bottom*), 19, 20 (*top*); Illustrated
London News: p 16 (*top right*); Mirror Syndication: pp 26 (*top*), 27, 30 (*both*),
back cover; Moviestore: 5 (*top*); Novosti: p 7 (*top*), 9 (*both*), 10 (*bottom*); P.A.
Photos/David Cheskin: p 4 (*bottom*); P.A. Photos/Fiona Hanson: p 23 (*bottom*).

Front cover: Novosti

Illustrations by Michael Ogden

Printed in Hong Kong

Contents

Sporting superstars

A hundred years ago, most sportsmen and sportswomen were **amateur**. They played games or ran races without being paid. Most of them had ordinary jobs and they did sport in their spare time.

Blackburn Rovers in 1903. Even these top footballers had to leave work early on a Saturday, so that they could play for their first-division team.

Today, most athletes and sports stars are **professional**. They are paid to run, jump or play games. Some people say that top sports stars are paid too much. The cost of their wages pushes up the cost for fans who want to watch them.

Some sports stars become rich. Here, boxer Prince Naseem Hamed poses on his new car.

Sports stars have been popular throughout history. In Ancient Rome, some **chariot** racers and **gladiators** became famous. Chariot racing was hugely popular. People supported "the Greens" or "the Blues" – different chariot teams – just as nowadays people support Manchester United or Real Madrid.

▲ In Ancient Rome, thousands of people watched gladiators fight.

Today, we no longer have to sit in a **stadium** to see champion athletes. We have TV, which shows us sporting events from all over the world. We have newspapers and magazines which tell us all about our sporting heroes and heroines.

USPGA tour

LASTMONTH

Tiger makes world event his own

On top: Tiger Woods destroyed the game's best players to win the Williams World Challenge

Tiger Woods was back to his destructive best in the final round of his own...

Woods' golf was brilliant as he one-putted nine holes in a row. There are now...

When he was 16 he became the youngest person to make...

The golden years

Edwards still out in front, but new kids are hovering

NEIL WILSON reports from Edmonton

JONATHAN Edwards put the pretenders of the next generation in their place here and pondered on the future at an age when most athletes have only a past.

His longest in three years — maintained the natural order in the triple jump and restored to him the world title that he won memorably in Gothenburg with two world record jumps.

But it was very different in Edmonton's Commonwealth Stadium. Gone were the hordes of his own generation, the Kenny Harrisons, the Denis Kapustins. Edwards, 35, was surrounded, deep in youth, by silver medallist Christian Olsson, 21, and bronze medallist Igor Spasovkhodski, 22. It was enough to make any man...

Stepping it up: Edwards makes his winning jump and then drinks to his success

Pictures ALLSPORT

games in Athens in 2004 he will not, probably cannot, say.

then for the 17.47m jump he had achieved and for the silver medal.

— my faith and my family. Nothing shakes that or ever will.

This book looks at some of the men and women who, through their sporting talents and their personalities, can truly be called sporting superstars.

Olga Korbut – *the world's favourite*

Olga Korbut was never the greatest gymnast. She did not win the most medals. But she was one of the most popular sportswomen in the world and she inspired millions of girls and boys to take up gymnastics.

Training

Korbut was born in 1955 in Belarus, which used to be part of the **USSR**. She was the youngest of four sisters. At junior school she was the smallest girl in the class, but she was better at running and jumping than anyone else. When she was eight, she joined a special sports school run by the great gymnastics coach, Renald Knysh.

Gymnastic events

vault

beam

asymmetric bars

parallel bars

floor exercise

The Korbut Salto (on the beam)

National championships

In 1969, Korbut competed in the national championships. The audience was astonished when she performed two new moves: a backwards somersault in the air (now called a Korbut Salto) on the beam, and a backwards flip (now called the Korbut Flip) on the asymmetric bars. Nobody had thought these moves were possible.

The Korbut Flip (on the asymmetric bars)

Olympic fame

In 1972, Korbut was chosen for the Olympic team. She trained hard but just five days before the team went to Munich she stopped practising her floor exercise. She did not like the moves and refused to do them.

Her coaches sat up all night working out a new set of moves. Korbut liked the new exercise and she practised hard.

The first gymnastics events at the Olympics were team events, where each gymnast scored points that counted to a team total. When Korbut performed her backwards flip on the **asymmetric bars**, the audience in the hall were thrilled by her daring and skill. The flip was shown on TV and the sports journalists agreed that no gymnast in history had ever performed such a move.

Korbut's performance in Munich soon caught the attention of the television cameras.

The next day, disaster struck. As Korbut jumped up onto the asymmetric bars, she made a mistake, which ruined her concentration and her rhythm. Her low score on the bars meant that she could not win a medal for the all-round event.

Everyone felt sorry for Korbut, who had tried so hard. Her coach, Renald Knysh, told her not to worry as there were still the individual events the following day.

The next day, Olga performed her routine on the asymmetric bars again for the individual medal. This time she performed perfectly. The judges gave her a score of 9.8 – a tie for the silver medal. The audience was angry. Most people thought the score should have been high enough to win the **gold**. The audience shouted and protested for nearly 25 minutes!

On the beam, Korbut gave another perfect performance. The judges gave her a score of 9.9 – and the gold medal.

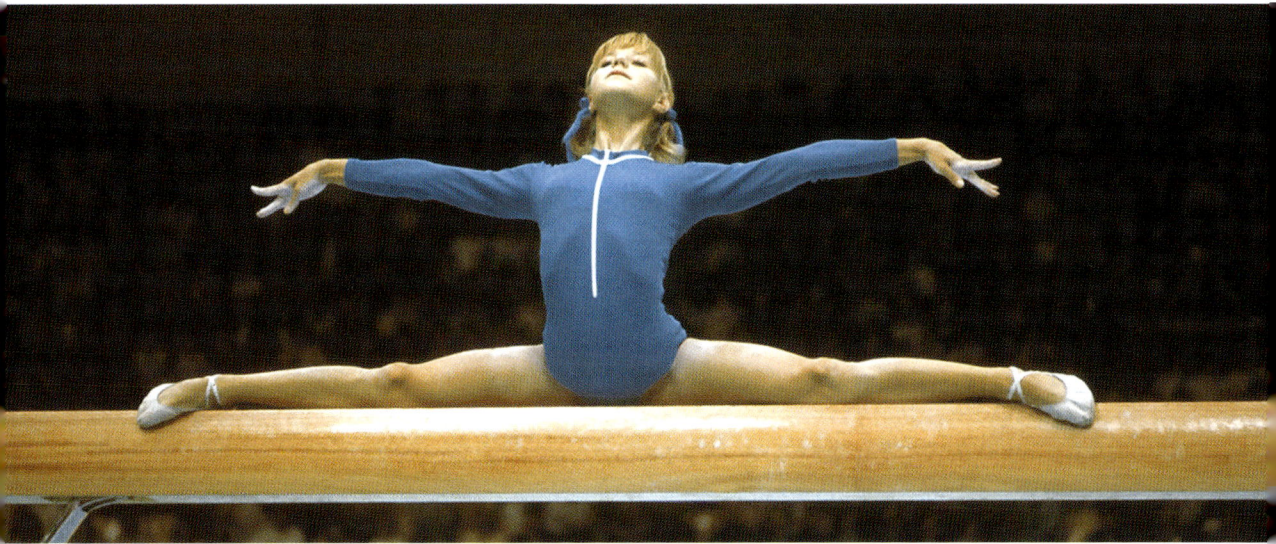

The floor exercise was the last event. This was the exercise that Korbut had learned just two weeks before. In an amazing display of gymnastics, Korbut gave the performance of her life and won the gold medal with a score of 9.9.

After amazing performances on the beam, bars and floor, Olga Korbut, just 17, became world-famous.

After the games, the **USSR** women's gymnastics team toured Europe and the USA. Korbut continued to train and enter competitions but suffered a bad ankle injury.

In the 1976 Olympics in Montreal, Korbut was unable to perform many of her famous moves, but she had massive support from the audience.

When she was given her silver medal, Korbut was given a louder, longer cheer than the gold-medal winner!

When Olga Korbut retired from gymnastics, she became a gymnastics teacher and a competition judge. In 1991, she and her family went to live in the USA.

Olga Korbut trains a new generation of young gymnasts. She has been called "The Mother of Modern Women's Gymnastics".

Mark Spitz – *the seven gold medal man*

Mark Spitz was a swimmer from the USA. He took part in his first Olympics at the age of 18. In the 1968 Games in Mexico, he was disappointed when he won "only" two **gold** medals in **relay** events.

Four years later, having trained hard, Spitz was ready for the 1972 Olympics in Munich. He won seven gold medals and set a new world record in each event.

Seven Golds for Spitz

- 100 m **freestyle**
- 200 m freestyle
- 100 m **butterfly**
- 200 m butterfly
- 4 x 100 m freestyle relay
- 4 x 200 m freestyle relay
- 4 x 100 m **medley** relay

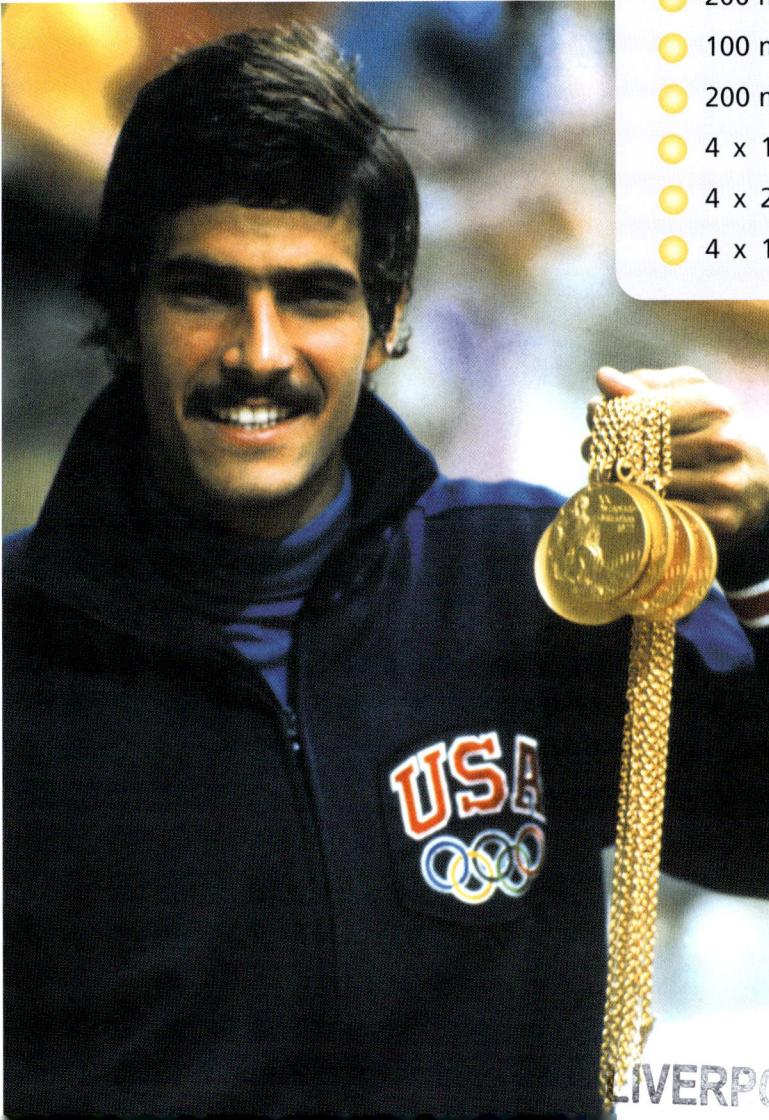

Spitz holds five of the seven gold medals he won in the Munich Olympics.

Paavo Nurmi – *the flying Finn*

In the three Olympic Games held in the 1920s, Paavo Nurmi won nine **gold** and three silver medals. He still holds the record for the most Olympic medals won by an athlete.

In 1924, he won the 1500 m and the 5000 m in the same afternoon!

The Medals

Antwerp Olympics (1920)

- 10,000 m – gold
- Cross-country – gold (individual)
- Cross-country – gold (team)
- 5000 m – silver

Paris Olympics (1924)

- 1500 m – gold
- 5000 m – gold
- Cross-country – gold (individual)
- Cross-country – gold (team)
- 3000 m – gold (team)

Amsterdam Olympics (1928)

- 10,000 m – gold
- 5000 m – silver
- 3000 m steeplechase – silver

"When he came through the archway leading to the track, we shouted a welcome to him that became deafening when he broke the tape.

Nurmi's time was 32 minutes 55 seconds. I am sure that no other living man could have done that. He is the wonder of all athletic ages."

▲ *Nurmi (on the wall) runs in the cross-country race in the Paris Olympics in 1924.*

▲ *A report in the* Daily Telegraph, *12 July 1924, describes Nurmi's cross-country win in the Paris Olympics.*

At the age of 55, Nurmi carried the Olympic torch into the stadium in his own country of Finland, to open the 1952 Olympic Games.

▲ *Nurmi opens the Olympic Games in Finland, 1952.*

Muhammad Ali – *"The Greatest"*

In the 1962 Olympics, a young boxer from the USA, called Cassius Clay, won the **gold** medal in the light-heavyweight boxing competition. He was so pleased with his medal that he wore it for months afterwards – until the gold finish on the medal wore away!

In 1964, Clay beat the world heavyweight champion Sonny Liston. Many people thought Liston was unbeatable, but before the match, Clay had boasted that he would win. Some people called Clay "The Mouth".

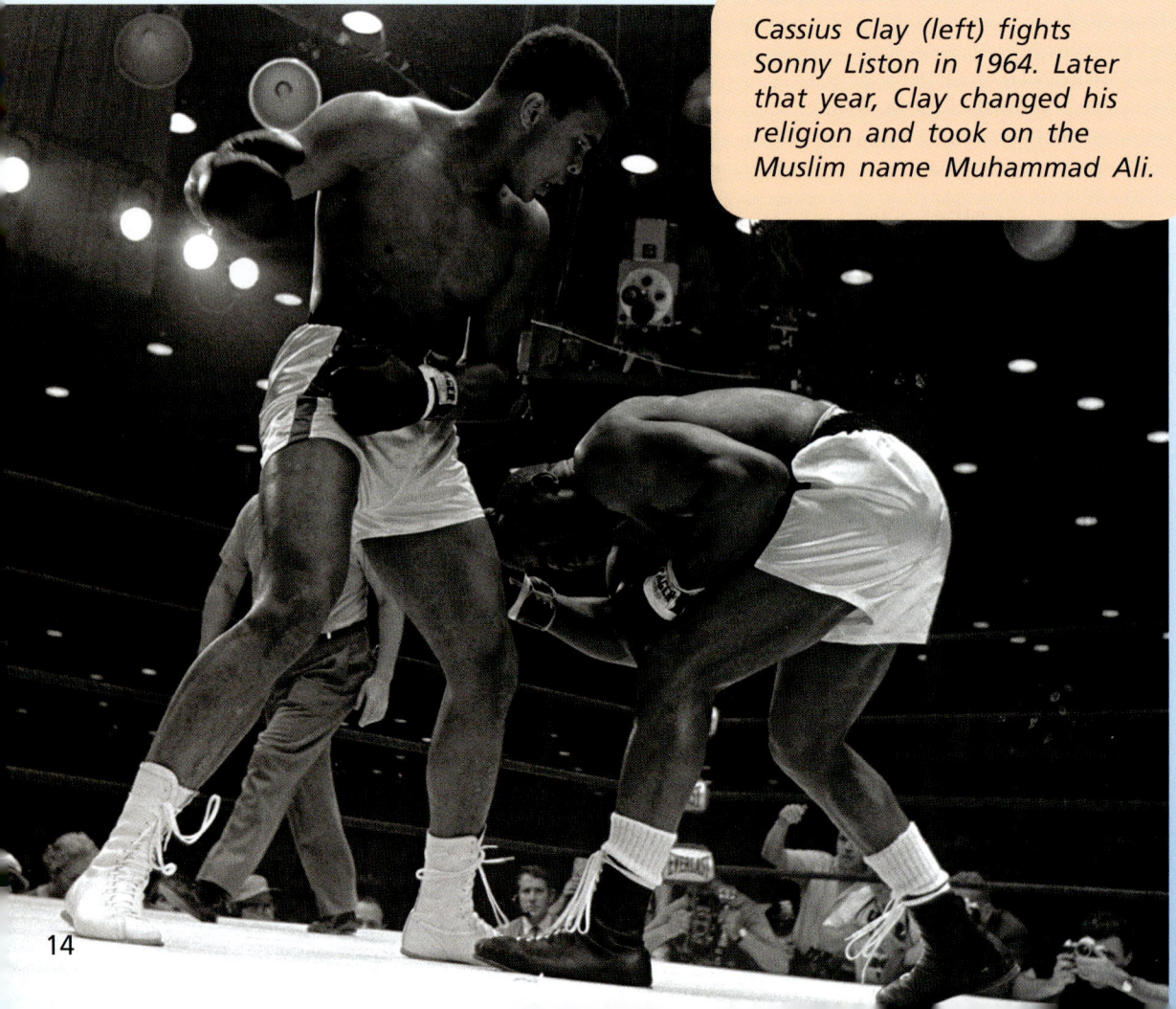

Cassius Clay (left) fights Sonny Liston in 1964. Later that year, Clay changed his religion and took on the Muslim name Muhammad Ali.

Muhammad Ali called himself "The Greatest". Many people think he was.

Even people who did not like boxing admired Muhammad Ali's skill and **stamina**. He boasted that he could "fly like a butterfly and sting like a bee" – and he could! When he was fighting, his agility and speed made him "fly" around the ring. His "sting" was a quick, sharp punch from either hand.

Muhammad Ali was the only man to win the world heavyweight championship three times.

Ali (right) defeats Jerry Quarry in the ring in 1970. After his ban from boxing, Ali proved that he had not lost any of his strength or skill.

In 1967, Ali was **stripped** of his title and banned from boxing, when he refused to join the American army fighting in the Vietnam War. He felt that the war was wrong. It was nearly four years before Muhammad Ali was allowed to box again.

Jesse Owens –
the man who upset Hitler

The 1936 Olympic Games took place in Adolf Hitler's Germany. Hitler tried to use the Games to get more support for his ideas and his political party – the Nazis.

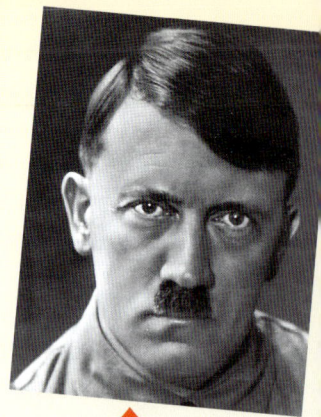

Jesse Owens

Adolf Hitler

Hitler believed white people were better than other people. He thought that white athletes would win all the big events. A young black American athlete, Jesse Owens, showed how wrong Hitler was.

Jesse Owens was a natural runner. As a child he shone at sports. At one school sports day he even equalled the world record of 9.4 seconds for the 100 yard (91.4 m) sprint.

In the streets of Berlin there were more Nazi flags than Olympic flags.

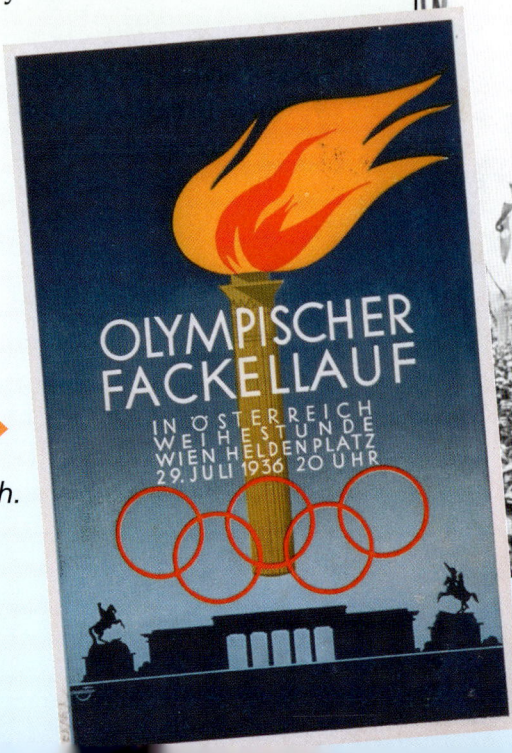

A poster from 1936, showing the Olympic torch.

OLYMPISCHER FACKELLAUF
IN ÖSTERREICH
WEIHESTUNDE
WIEN HELDENPLATZ
29. JULI 1936 20 UHR

Owens came from a poor family and had to work hard to support himself as a student. He joined the college athletics team and broke world records for running, long jump and hurdles.

In 1936, Owens was given a place in the USA team for the Olympics in Berlin.

The 100 m gold medal

Jesse's first Olympic event was the 100 m. In the second **heat**, Owens broke the world record with a time of 10.2 seconds. In the final, he equalled the Olympic record of 10.3 seconds and won the **gold** medal.

Owens breaks the world long-jump record in 1935.

Owens crosses the finishing line in the 100 m, and wins his first Olympic gold medal.

Next, in the first two heats of the 200 m, Owens twice broke the Olympic record. The winners of the heats had a day's rest before the final. But Owens had no rest because he was in the long jump.

The long-jump gold medal

Owens knew he was the fastest runner in the world, but he was not sure he could do so well in the long jump. His mind was changed by a new friend, the German long-jump champion, Luz Long.

A few German athletes tried to keep alive the Olympic ideal of friendly competition. Luz Long was one of these athletes. He did not believe Hitler's ideas about different races and he became great friends with Jesse Owens.

Luz Long was hot favourite with the German crowds to win the long jump, but Jesse Owens held the world record. Both men were determined to win, but they still encouraged each other to do their best.

Luz Long and Jesse Owens were friends even though they competed against each other.

On the day of the event, Luz Long jumped 7.87 m, breaking the previous Olympic record. But then Jesse Owens jumped an incredible 8.06 m.

▲
*Owens' jump wins him the **gold** medal and sets a new Olympic and world record.*

Hitler left the Olympic **stadium**. He was furious that a black American had beaten the German champion.

Friends and rivals

Years later, Owens wrote about his friendship with Luz Long.

"We grew to be fast friends through the Games. Hitler or no Hitler, he gave me one of the hardest battles I ever had in athletics. When I made my final record-breaking jump, Luz Long was the first to congratulate me – and he meant it."

The 200 m gold medal

The next day, Owens won the final of the 200 m in 20.7 seconds, breaking his own record, which he set in the second-round heats.

Owens starts the 200 m final in which he set a new Olympic record.

The 400 m relay gold medal

Four days later, running the first **leg** of the 4 x 100 m **relay**, Jesse Owens made sure that the American team broke the world record. He won his fourth Olympic **gold** medal.

Through the Games, Jesse Owens broke or equalled twelve Olympic records. He also smashed Hitler's dream that white athletes would win all the big events.

In later life, Jesse Owens started the Jesse Owens Foundation, which gave money and support to help poor young people to succeed.

In the lead, Owens takes the baton from his team-mate in the relay.

Martina Navratilova –
Wimbledon wonder

Martina Navratilova was born in Eastern Europe, in the country that is now called the Czech Republic. She is the most successful woman tennis player the world has ever known.

Fact box

Navratilova dominated women's tennis for more than 10 years.

- In 1983 and 1984, she won more prize money than any other sports star.
- In 1990, she won her *ninth* Wimbledon women's final.
- By the time she retired in 1994, she had won a record-breaking 167 championship tennis titles.

Navratilova wins her first Wimbledon trophy in 1978.

Tennis is played all over the world and there are tennis competitions in many countries. The game began in England and, for many players and fans, the most important event each year is the tennis championship held at Wimbledon, London.

Mary Peters – *pride of Northern Ireland*

At the 1972 Olympics in Munich, Mary Peters, from Northern Ireland, won the women's pentathlon with a world record-breaking score. Her total score was 4801. It was ten points more than her closest rival.

The pentathlon is one of the hardest tests for women athletes, because it is made up of five different events.

The pentathlon events

60 m hurdles

high jump

long jump

800 m running

shot put

Points are awarded for an athlete's performance in each event. The winner is the athlete with the highest total of points.

It was the third time that Peters had competed in the Olympics. She was only the third British woman to win an athletics Olympic **gold**. It was a fantastic win because she won the gold medal at the age of 33. She had been competing in the pentathlon since the age of 16!

Mary Peters went on to be a successful **sports administrator**. She became President of the British Athletics Association in 1996 and worked hard organizing sporting events for the disabled.

The 200 m race was the final event in the pentathlon. Peters (left) came fourth, but that gave her enough points to win the pentathlon gold medal.

In 2000, Peters was given an award and a title, by the Queen, for her work. She is now "Dame Mary Peters".

23

Linford Christie – *Europe's best sprinter*

Linford Christie was born in Jamaica in 1960. When he was still a baby, his family moved to Britain. He grew up in South London. Even at primary school he was a fast runner.

When he was a teenager, sports writers were predicting that he would be a future champion. He entered his first international competition at the age of 20.

From 1980 to 1997, Christie ran for Britain in over 60 international competitions. During that time, he won more championship medals than any other British male athlete.

Christie was the first European to run 100 m in less than ten seconds. ▶

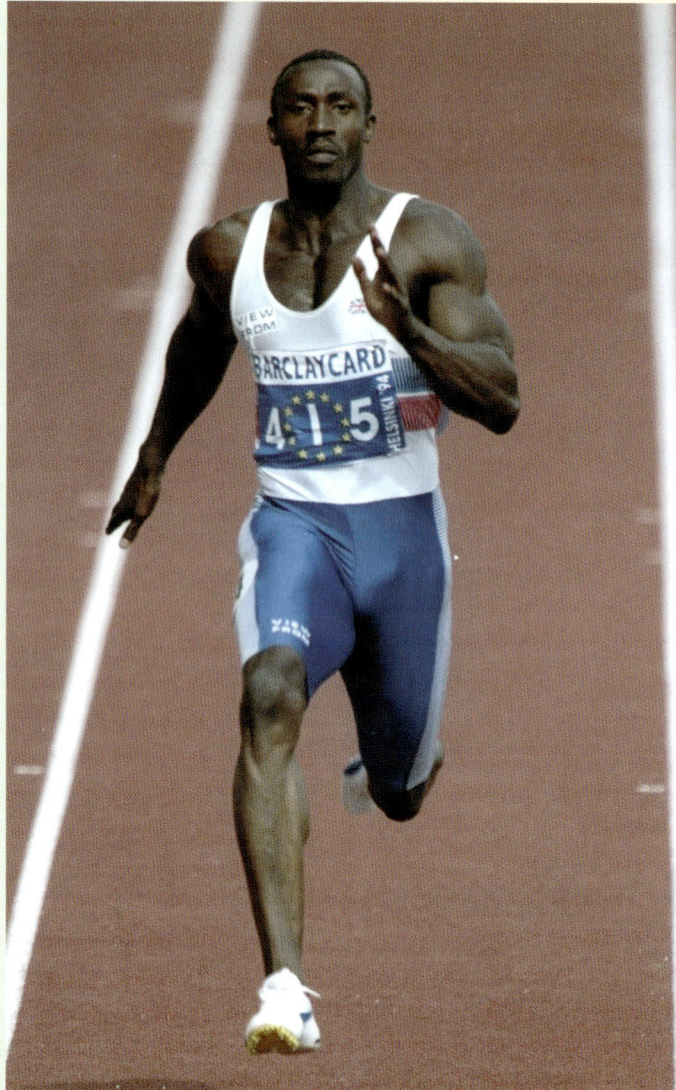

His best event was the 100 m and he won many 100 m races in European and World championships.

In 1992, at the Olympic Games in Barcelona, Christie won the **gold** medal in the 100 m at the age of 32. He was the oldest man ever to win the Olympic 100 m.

First across the finishing line, Christie wins the 100 m at the Olympics in 1992.

"*I was running scared,*" said Linford Christie after the race. "*I run with a controlled fear of losing. When you are frightened in that way it's amazing what you can achieve.*"

In 1995, Christie broke the world indoor record for the 200 m with a time of 20.25 seconds. Two years later, Christie retired from running.

Since he retired, Christie has trained many young athletes. He has also made appearances on TV, as a sports **commentator** and as a presenter of children's programmes.

25

Steve Redgrave – *twenty years at the top*

Steve Redgrave is a rower. He is the only British athlete ever to win **gold** medals at five Olympic Games.

Redgrave trained hard to stay at the top of his sport. He had diabetes and other illnesses, but he followed a tough training schedule of five hours a day, seven days a week, for over twenty years.

▲ *Redgrave training on the River Thames.*

Gold medal 1

His first gold was in the **Coxed Fours** in Los Angeles in 1984.

Gold medal 2

His second gold was for the **Coxless Pairs** at Seoul in 1988, with Andy Holmes.

Gold medal 3

His third gold was for the Coxless Pairs at the Barcelona Olympics in 1992, with Matthew Pinsent.

Redgrave and Pinsent celebrate their win at the Barcelona Olympics, 1992. ▶

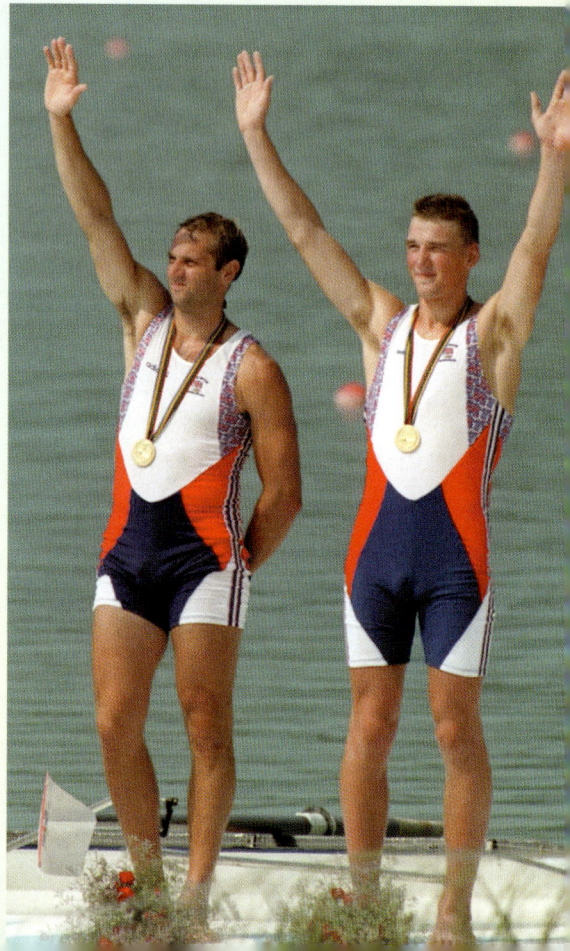

Gold medal 4

His fourth gold was again for the Coxless Pairs with Matthew Pinsent at the Atlanta Olympics in 1996. After the race, Redgrave said that he was going to retire. He said that if anyone saw him near a boat again they could shoot him!

Gold medal 5

Redgrave took a break from training, but he did not retire. He was back rowing in the 2000 Sydney Olympics.

Redgrave and his team in the semi-final at the Sydney Olympics, 2000.

On 23 September 2000, more than 7.5 million people sat up late to watch Redgrave on TV, competing for his fifth Olympic gold medal in the Coxless Fours. His team-mates were Matthew Pinsent, Tim Foster and James Cracknell.

They won the race and Redgrave got his fifth gold medal. (Pinsent got his third, and Foster and Cracknell got their first.)

Redgrave was asked what he felt about all the gold medals. He said,

"The first is the best, but every one is special and every one is different."

Akebono – *the mighty outsider*

Athletes are usually slim. But there are some sports, like weight-lifting and heavyweight boxing, where size and weight are very important. One of the most surprising sporting superstars is a very big and very heavy man from Hawaii called Akebono. He is 2.04 m tall and he weighs around 225 kg.

Akebono at the opening ceremony of the Winter Olympics, 1998.

Sumo wrestling is not a sport that is well known, except in Japan. The sport is very popular in Japan and is often on TV. Sumo wrestlers have their own fan clubs and the national championships are big news in Japan.

Sumo wrestling was invented in Japan and, since the sport began, every Sumo wrestler has come from Japan – except Akebono.

Akebono's real name is Chad Rowan and he was born in Hawaii, USA. As a young man, he became interested in becoming a Sumo wrestler but he found that all Sumo wrestlers were from Japan. No outsider had ever even tried to be a Sumo wrestler.

However, Rowan joined a Sumo school. He learned to speak Japanese. He trained hard and his teachers were forced to admit that this outsider had great ability in the skills of Sumo. Rowan went on to win many fights. He has a lot of fans.

In 2000, after winning the national championships, Akebono was awarded the title of "Yokozuna". This is the highest rank of Sumo wrestler.

In Sumo wrestling, the two wrestlers fight in a small round ring. One of the ways to score points is to lift or push your opponent out of the ring.

judge

Akebono

ring

David Beckham – *love him or laugh at him*?

David Beckham is a great footballer. Even as a boy, he showed great talent and as soon as he left school he joined Manchester United football club.

Playing mainly on the right wing, Beckham shows his brilliance whenever he takes a corner or a free kick. Many people believe that he is the best in the world at crossing a ball – kicking the ball across the pitch so that it lands in the best possible place for other players in his team.

Some people laugh at Beckham because of his London accent. When he wrote a book some people laughed because most of the book was photos. But clever or not, Beckham is rich, successful and happy.

Are the people who laugh at him just jealous?

Superstars, such as Beckham and his family, are often in the news. Fame can bring danger as well as money.

WORLD EXCLUSIVE

PLOT TO KIDNAP BABY BECKS

By IAN HYLAND

A SHOCKING plot to hold the baby of David and Victoria Beckham to ransom has been dramatically foiled by police.

The kidnappers planned to snatch baby Brooklyn and possibly Posh Spice before demanding a fortune for their safe return.

Officers went undercover to infiltrate the gang but police were so worried about the threat that the superstar couple and Brooklyn were moved to a safe house, along with Victoria's family.

When police feared the kidnappers were about to make their move, Victoria was told by detectives: "We've got to get you out of here."

● FULL STORY: Pages 2, 3, 4 & 5 ● POSH'S BUST OP: Pages 12 & 13 ● UNITE

TARGETS: Victoria Beckham and baby Brooklyn this week. They were

Wednesday, November 24, 1999

Ireland's brightest paper

Irish Mirror

EDITED AND PRINTED IN IRELAND   IT'S ALL ABOUT YOU

40p

CHAMPIONS LEAGUE
Fiorentina....2
Man Utd......0
SEE BACK PAGE

Why is Beckham as clever as Einstein?

SEE PAGE 6

Glossary

amateur (in sport) person who takes part without payment

asymmetric bars two bars which are not the same height

butterfly (in sport) swimming style where both arms swing round the head then through the water

chariot small horse-drawn cart

commentator person who describes a sport or game to TV or radio audiences

coxed fours four rowers in a boat, with one extra person (the cox) directing the boat

coxless pairs two rowers in a boat who steer themselves

freestyle (in swimming) any style the swimmer chooses

gladiator professional fighter in Ancient Rome.

gold in sport, the colour of the medal for winning the event (silver for 2nd; bronze for 3rd)

heat one of a series of races before the main race or other event to decide which athletes go through to the final

leg (of a relay) the distance that one runner has to run in a relay race before handing the baton to the next runner

medley (in swimming) a relay race where different swimmers swim in different styles

professional (in sport) person who takes part for payment

relay race run by teams of athletes. Each athlete in a team runs part of the race. Often a wooden stick or baton is passed from each runner to the next.

sports administrator an official who organizes and supervises sporting events

stadium place specially built for sports (e.g. football stadium)

stamina the ability to keep going

stripped (of a title) having a sporting title taken away by sports administrators, rather than losing the title by being beaten by another athlete or sports person

USSR The Union of Soviet Socialist Republics, also called the Soviet Union. This was a group of countries, under one government led by Russia. In the late 1990s, the USSR broke up into separate countries ruling themselves.

Index of people

526521

Index of sports